The Little Old MacDonald's Farm

Coloring Book

Anna Pomaska

Dover Publications, Inc., New York

Published in Canada by General Publishing Company, Ltd., 30 Lesmill Road, Don Mills, Toronto, Ontario.
Published in the United Kingdom by Constable and Company, Ltd., 10 Orange Street, London WC2H 7EG.

The Little Old MacDonald's Farm Coloring Book is a new work, first published by Dover Publications, Inc., in 1986.

International Standard Book Number: 0-486-25159-4

Manufactured in the United States of America
Dover Publications, Inc., 31 East 2nd Street,
Mineola, N.Y. 11501

Everyone loves to sing the song "Old Mac-Donald Had a Farm." Now, with this book, you can visit Old MacDonald's farm, and you can have as much fun coloring all the delightful characters you meet there as you have when you sing about them. Here are wonderful drawings of everyone's favorite farmer, Old MacDonald himself, and of all his friendly farm animals. Stop by and see the mother hen and her chicks; the big, fat pig and the plump little piglets; the happy cows and calves; the baby ducks and their mother; the horses and the colt; and all the other animals that live on the farm. As you color the pictures, you'll also be sure to enjoy reading about Old MacDonald and his animals. Find out what they like to do on the farm and what sounds they make. If, while you are coloring or reading, you suddenly get the urge to join Old MacDonald in song, then just turn to page 61 for all the words and music to "Old MacDonald Had a Farm." All together now: "E-I-E-I-O!"

This is Old MacDonald. He is a farmer. He likes to sing "E-I-E-I-O!" as he works on the farm.

"E-I-E-I-O!"

On the farm there is a big red barn where some of the farm animals live.

"Moo, moo!" "Neigh, neigh!"   7

The rooster crows in the morning
and wakes up Old MacDonald
with a "Cock-a-doodle-doo!"

"Cock-a-doodle-doo!" 9

The mother hen lays eggs and
keeps them warm by sitting
on them. She clucks happily while
waiting for her chicks to hatch.

"Cluck, cluck!"

When the chicks hatch, they say
"Chick, chick!" Later, when the
mother hen finds something good
to eat, she calls her chicks:
"Cluck, cluck!"

"Chick, chick!"

"Chick, chick!"

"Cluck, cluck!" "Chick, chick!"

On the farm there is a big, fat
pig and there are also some plump
little piglets. They all say "Oink,
oink," especially when they have
something good to eat.

"Oink, oink!"

"Oink, oink!"

"Oink, oink!"

"Oink, oink!"

"Oink, oink!"

Old MacDonald milks the cows.
Then the cows join the calves out
in the pasture where they all eat
grass and moo happily.

"Moo, moo!" "E-I-E-I-O!"

"Moo, moo!"

"Moo, moo!"

On the farm there are some dogs.
They like to run around, dig
holes and bury bones. Most of
all, they enjoy playing in the
pasture with the cows and
barking "Bowwow!"

"Bowwow!"

"Bowwow!"

"Bowwow!"

"Bowwow!"

"Moo, moo!"

The baby ducks stay close to
their mother when they go for a
walk and when they take a swim.
"Quack, quack!" is what they
all say when they are having a
good time.

"Quack, quack!"

34   "Quack, quack!"

"Quack, quack!"

The sheep all say "Baa, baa!"
The father sheep has big curved
horns and a thick woolly coat. The
little lambs like to play with each
other in the meadow.

"Baa, baa!"

"Baa, baa!"

"Baa, baa!"

The donkey likes to kick up his heels and hee-haw. Sometimes Old MacDonald has the donkey pull a cart.

"Hee-haw!"

On the farm there is a cat. She
and her four kittens like to meow
all the time. The cat's job is to
hunt for mice, and the kittens
have fun playing with a ball of
yarn.

"Meow, meow!"

"Meow, meow!"

"Meow, meow!"

On the farm there is a big goose
that honks very loudly. All her
little goslings follow her as if they
were in a parade.

"Honk, honk!"

Old MacDonald's horses like to eat hay in the barn and grass in the meadow. The young colt loves to run all over and neigh to his parents, who are always close by.

"Neigh, neigh!"

"Neigh, neigh!"

"Neigh, neigh!"

51

The father goat has big horns and a long beard. The kids do not have large horns yet, but they like to pretend they do when they play. They all say "Naa, naa!"

"Naa, naa!"

"Naa, naa!"

"Naa, naa!"

On the farm there is a fat turkey that eats a lot of corn. He is very proud of his beautiful feathers. He is always gobbling so that everyone will look at him as he struts around the farm.

Verse 5

And on this farm he had some cows, E-I-E-I-O!
With a moo, moo here, and a moo, moo there,
Here a moo, there a moo, everywhere a moo, moo.
Oink, oink here, and an oink, oink there,
Here an oink, there an oink, everywhere an oink, oink.
Cluck, cluck here, and a cluck, cluck there,
Here a cluck, there a cluck, everywhere a cluck, cluck.
Quack, quack here, and a quack, quack there,
Here a quack, there a quack, everywhere a quack, quack.
Chick, chick here, and a chick, chick there,
Here a chick, there a chick, everywhere a chick, chick.
Old MacDonald had a farm, E-I-E-I-O!

Additional verses may be added following this same pattern. The other animals on Old MacDonald's farm in this book are:

6. Dogs
With a bowwow here, and a bowwow there,
Here a bow, there a wow, everywhere a bowwow.

7. Sheep
With a baa, baa here, and a baa, baa there,
Here a baa, there a baa, everywhere a baa, baa.

8. Donkey
With a hee-haw here, and a hee-haw there,
Here a hee, there a haw, everywhere a hee-haw.

9. Cats:
With a meow, meow here, and a meow, meow there,
Here a meow, there a meow, everywhere a meow, meow.

10. Geese
With a honk, honk here, and a honk, honk there,
Here a honk, there a honk, everywhere a honk, honk.

11. Horses
With a neigh, neigh here, and a neigh, neigh there,
Here a neigh, there a neigh, everywhere a neigh, neigh.

12. Goats
With a naa, naa here, and a naa, naa there,
Here a naa, there a naa, everywhere a naa, naa.

13. Turkey
With a gobble, gobble here, and a gobble, gobble there,
Here a gobble, there a gobble, everywhere a gobble, gobble.

14. Rooster
With a cock-a-doodle-doo here, and a cock-a-doodle-doo there,
Here a cock-a-doodle, there a doodle-doo, everywhere a cock-a-doodle-doo.

"Gobble, gobble!" 57

Sing along with us!

59

Old MacDonald Had a Farm

(part one)

Old Mac-Don-ald had a farm, E - I - E - I - O!

(part two)

1. And on this farm he had some chicks, E - I - E - I - O! With a
2. And on this farm he had some ducks, E - I - E - I - O! With a

(part three)

Chick, chick here, and a chick, chick there,
Quack, quack here, and a quack, quack there,

Here a chick, there a chick, Eve-ry where a chick, chick.
Here a quack, there a quack, Eve-ry where a quack, quack.

(part four)

Old Mac-Don-ald had a farm, E - I - E - I - O!

Verses of "Old MacDonald Had a Farm"

Verse 3

And on this farm he had some hens, E-I-E-I-O!
With a cluck, cluck here, and a cluck, cluck there,
Here a cluck, there a cluck, everywhere a cluck, cluck.
Quack, quack here, and a quack, quack there,
Here a quack, there a quack, everywhere a quack, quack.
Chick, chick here, and a chick, chick there,
Here a chick, there a chick, everywhere a chick, chick.
Old MacDonald had a farm, E-I-E-I-O!

Verse 4

And on this farm he had some pigs, E-I-E-I-O!
With an oink, oink here, and an oink, oink there,
Here an oink, there an oink, everywhere an oink, oink.
Cluck, cluck here, and a cluck, cluck there,
Here a cluck, there a cluck, everywhere a cluck, cluck.
Quack, quack here, and a quack, quack there,
Here a quack, there a quack, everywhere a quack, quack.
Chick, chick here, and a chick, chick there,
Here a chick, there a chick, everywhere a chick, chick.
Old MacDonald had a farm, E-I-E-I-O!